BEST OF GRAM PARSONS

CONTENTS

Cover photo by Corbis

Additional photos courtesy of Gretchen Carpenter

Special thanks to Gretchen and Robert Carpenter for overseeing this book

Piano/vocal arrangements by Andy Fitzpatrick

Cherry Lane Music Company
Director of Publications/Project Editor: Mark Phillips
Manager of Publications: Gabrielle Fastman

ISBN: 978-1-57560-954-6

Visit our website at www.cherrylane.com

FOREWORD

Gram's songs transcend time. They will forever remain in our hearts.

I spent two great years, 1969 and 1970, with this man in our band the Flying Burrito Brothers. We shared a common bond through love lost and new love found. Our emotions ran the gauntlet as we struggled to put our thoughts into words and our words into music.

We created a sound with the Burrito Brothers that has continued to inspire many who have followed in our footsteps. I will always cherish that special moment in time I spent with Gram Parsons and I will hold those memories dear for the rest of my life.

His legacy stands tall and proud, his music eternal.

—Chris Hillman
  2008

Blue Eyes

Written by
Gram Parsons

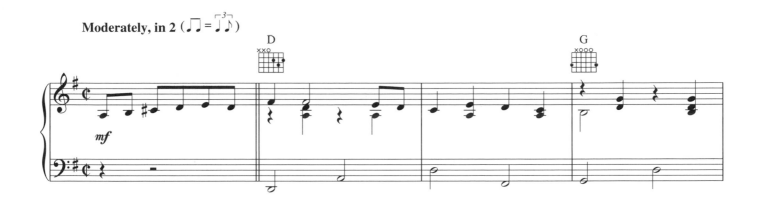

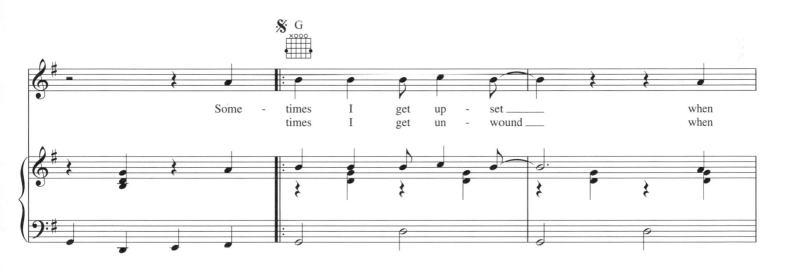

chores to keep me bus- y, a clock to keep my time, a pret- ty girl to love me with the same last name as mine. And when the flow- ers wilt, a big old quilt to keep us warm.

I've got the sun to see ___ your blue ___ eyes, and to-

To Coda night you're in my arms. |1. Some - |2. arms.

D.S. (lyric 2) al Coda Some - Coda arms.

6

Brass Buttons

Written by
Gram Parsons

To Coda

Oh, but

All ___ the time ___ ev -'ry - I think she knew. ___
I re - mem - ber thing she said. ___

1.
2.

D.S. al Coda

Brass

Coda

Christine's Tune

Words and Music by
Gram Parsons and Chris Hillman

She's a dev-il in dis-guise, _____ in dis-

guise.

Now, a wom-an like that, all she does __ is
hap - pi - ness has been her close __ com -
num - ber al - ways turns up in ___ your

hate you.
pan - ion.
pock - et

She does - n't know what
Her world is full of
when - ev - er you are

Do You Know How It Feels
to Be Lonesome

Written by
Gram Parsons

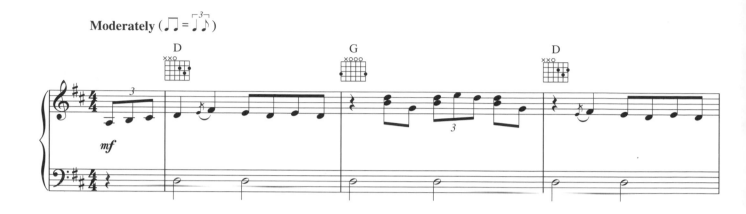

Do you know how it feels _____ to be

lone - some, ___ when there's just __ no one

left who real-ly cares? Did you ev-er try to smile at some peo-ple, and all they ev-er seem to do is stare? Can you re-mem-ber how it

To Coda

Drug Store Truck Drivin' Man

Words and Music by
Roger McGuinn and Gram Parsons

When sum-mer ___ rolls a - round,

he'll be luck-y if he's not in town. ___

Well, he's got him ___ a house on the
Well, he don't like ___ the young folks, I
He's been like ___ a fa - ther to

hill. ___ He plays coun-try rec-ords till
know. ___ He told me one night on his
me. ___ He's the on-ly D - J you can

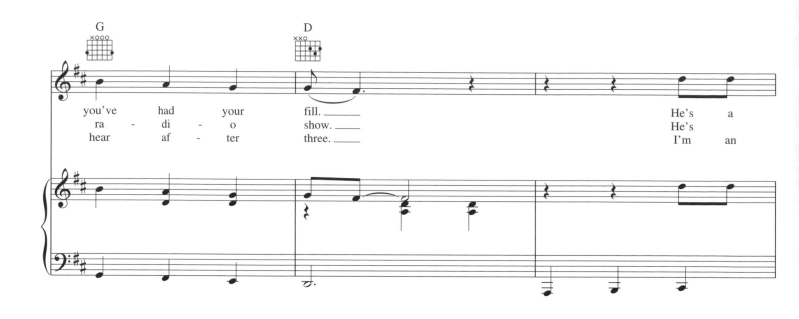

you've had your fill. _____
ra - di - o show. _____
hear af - ter three. _____

He's a
He's
I'm an

fire - man's friend; he's an all - night D - J. _____
got him a med - al he won in the war. _____
all - night mu - si - cian in a rock - and - roll band, _____

But he sure does think dif - f'rent from the
It weighs five hun - dred pounds and it
and why he don't like me I

Hickory Wind

Words and Music by
Gram Parsons and Bob Buchanan

Hot Burrito No. 1

(I'm Your Toy Horn)

Words and Music by
Gram Parsons and Chris Ethridge

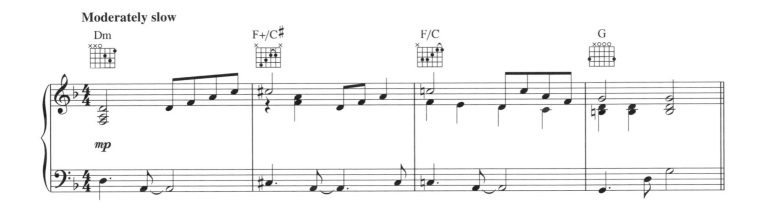

You may be sweet and nice, ___ but that won't keep you

warm ___ at night, 'cause I'm the one who showed you how

I'm your toy, I'm your old boy, _____ but I don't want

no one but you to love _____ me. No, I would-n't lie.

You know _ I'm not that kind of guy. _____

D.S. al Coda

kind of guy.

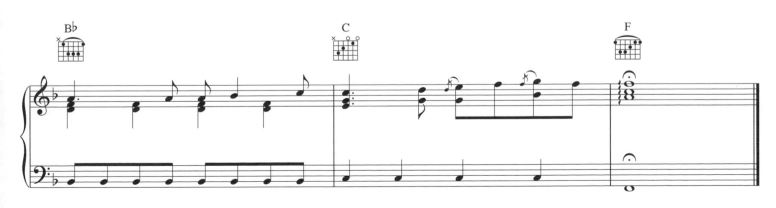

Hot Burrito No. 2

Words and Music by
Gram Parsons and Chris Ethridge

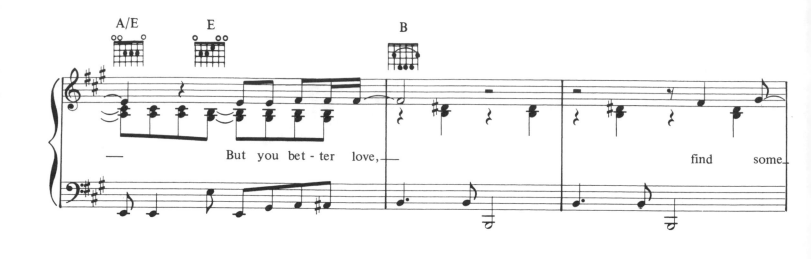

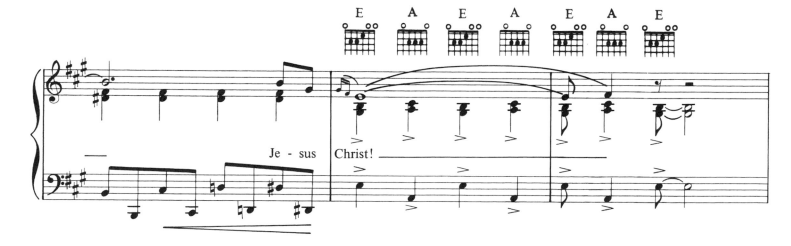

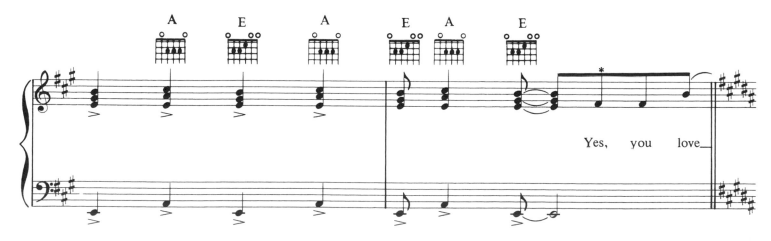

* Instrumental omitted

In My Hour of Darkness

Words and Music by
Emmylou Harris and Gram Parsons

miles and miles _____ with - out a word, with
played to peo - ple ev - 'ry - where; some
he read me _____ just like a book, and he

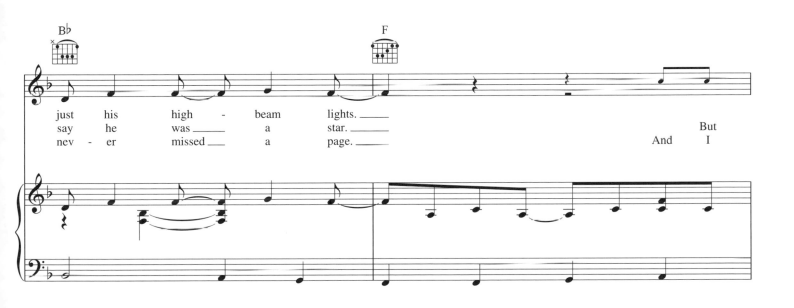

just his high - beam lights. _____
say he was _____ a star. _____ But
nev - er missed _____ a page. _____ And I

Who'd have ev - er thought _____ they'd build _____ such a
he was just _____ a coun - try boy, _____ his
loved him like _____ my fa - ther, and I

D.S. al Coda

Oh, Lord, grant me vi-

sion, oh, Lord, grant me speed.

100 Years from Now

Written by
Gram Parsons

Moderately bright

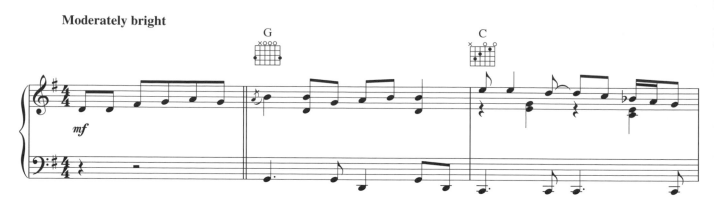

One _____ hun - dred
One _____ hun - dred

years __ from this day,
years __ from this time,

will the peo - ple _____ still
would an - y - bod - y

$1,000 Wedding

Written by
Gram Parsons

Moderately slow

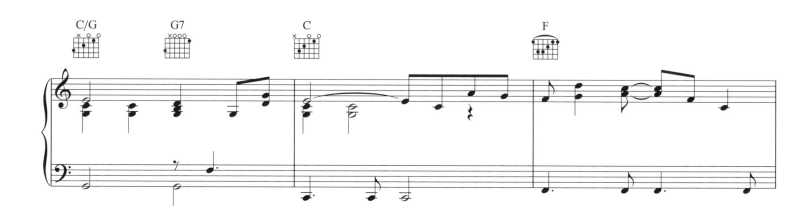

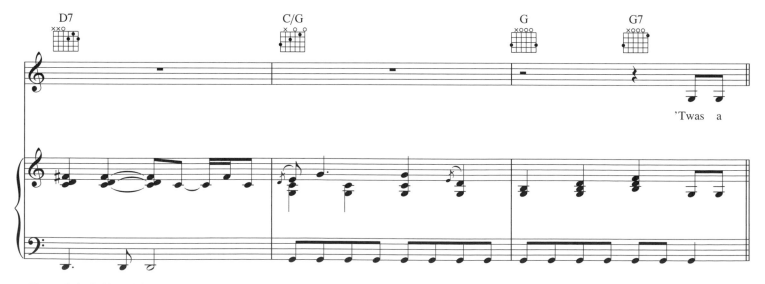

'Twas a

*Recorded a half step higher.

day.

The Rev-'rend Doc - tor Wil - liam Grace _____ was

talk - ing to _____ the crowd all _____ a - bout _ the sweet _ Child's _____

ho - ly face _____ and the saints who sung _ out loud. _____

Ooh, Las Vegas

Written by
Gram Parsons and Richard Grech

* Not the key of A, but a transposed mixolydian mode on E

Las Ve - gas ____ ain't no

place for a poor boy like me

Ev - 'ry time I hit your

crys - tal cit - ty I know ____ you're gon - na make a wreck ____ out - ta

Last time to Coda

55

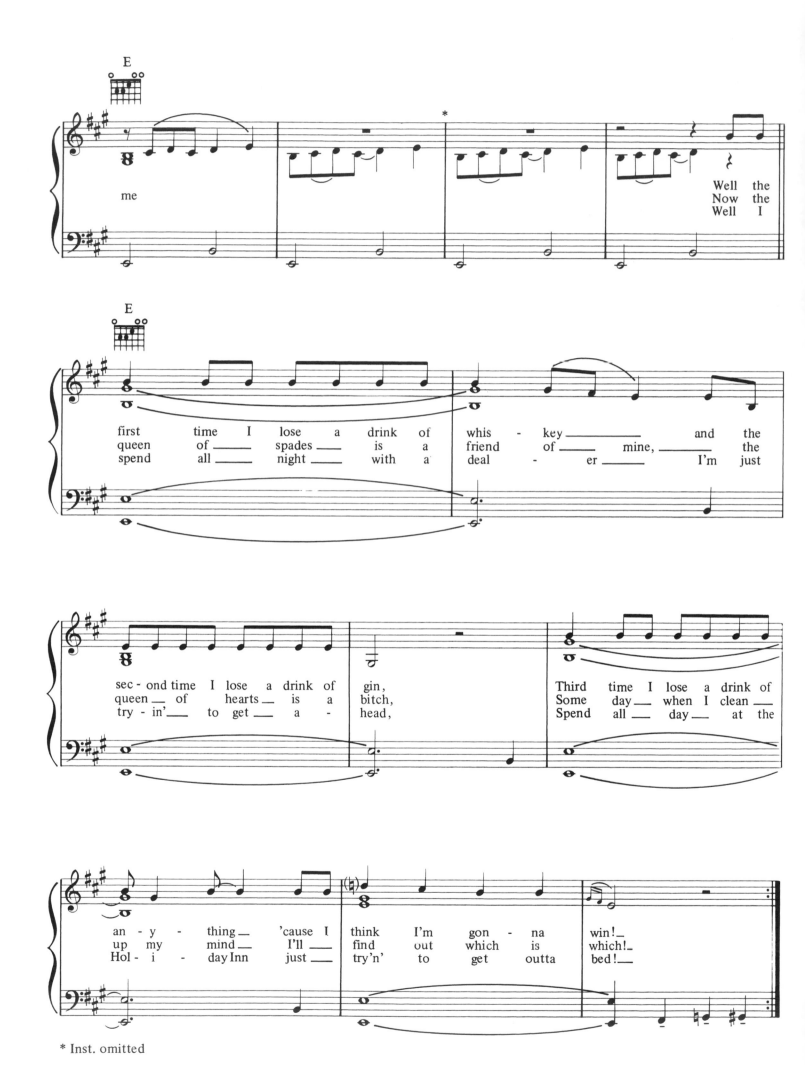

*Inst. omitted

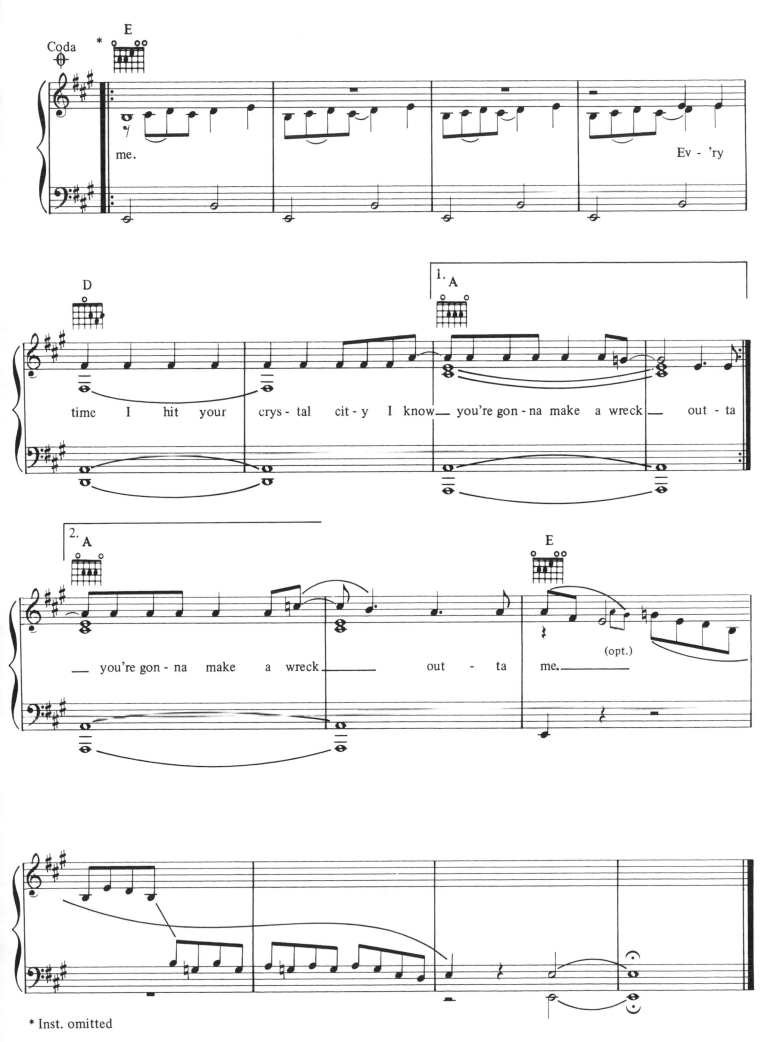

* Inst. omitted

Return of the Grievous Angel

Words and Music by
Thomas S. Brown and Gram Parsons

and I'll ___ be damned _ if it ___ did not ___ come true. _

___ Twen - ty thou - sand roads _

___ I went down, down, down, ___ and

they all led ___ me straight ___ back home ___ to you.

61

and I saw ___ my deep ___ blue sea. _____ And I

thought a - bout a cal - i - co bon - net   from Chey - enne to Ten - nes - see. ___

To Coda I

We flew straight _ a - cross that

riv - er bridge _ last night, half past two. ___   Switch-

man waved his lan - tern good - bye ___ and good day ___ as we went roll - ing through. ___

Bill - boards and truck - stops pass ___ by the griev - ous an -

gel, and now I know ___ just

D.S. al Coda I

what I have ___ to do. And the

Twen-ty thou-sand roads ___ I went down, ___ down, ___ down, ___ and they all led ___ me straight ___ back home ___ to you. ___

The

you.

D.S. al Coda II

64

A Song for You

Written by
Gram Parsons